The author and publishers would like to
thank Caroline Gaspard LCST and Caroline Harlow LCST for
their assistance in the preparation of this book.

First published in Great Britain 1983 by
Hamish Hamilton Children's Books
Garden House, 57–59 Long Acre, London WC2E 9JZ
Copyright © 1983 by Nigel Snell
All Rights Reserved

British Library Cataloguing in Publication Data

Snell, Nigel
Anne visits the speech therapist
I. Title
823′.914[J]   PZ7
ISBN 0 241 11029 7

Printed in Great Britain by
Cambus Litho, East Kilbride

Ann visits the Speech Therapist

NIGEL SNELL

Hamish Hamilton · London

Ann was very pretty.
She laughed a lot,
but she said things in a funny way.

Ann was rather unhappy.
She wondered why grandma
couldn't understand her.

One day, mummy took Ann
to see the doctor.
He tested her ears
and looked in her mouth.
'Nothing wrong there', he said.
'But I would like Ann to see a speech therapist.

Later that week, mummy took Ann
to the clinic.
They sat in a room with lots of
other girls and boys.

Soon a door opened.
The speech therapist called
mummy and Ann into her room.

The speech therapist was a nice lady.
Her name was Pam.
She sat on the floor with lots of toys
and played with Ann.

Ann had to bang three drums,
one after the other.
First she had to bang them slowly,
then quickly.
Soon it was time to go home.

Next week, Pam came to see Ann at home.
She brought a book with shapes
for Ann to colour,
and lots of other pictures.

Ann had to draw in the stems
of some flowers,
all the way down to the flower pots.
Pam talked to mummy for quite a long time.

The next time Ann went to the clinic,
she learnt her 'Mmm' for mummy sound.
She felt her lips to see what they were doing.
Pam had a tape recorder.
She allowed Ann to say something to it.
But it didn't talk back!

Sometimes, Pam shone a torch
in mummy's mouth so that Ann could see
what mummy's tongue was doing.
Ann watched mummy's lips
move together and say 'Mmm'.
She stood in front of the mirror
and tried it herself.

Ann learnt to say 'C' for cat,
and other sounds.
Ann watched her tongue
and lips in the mirror
to see if she was doing it right.

Ann went to the clinic
once a week and played.
Sometimes, she gave a dirty doll
a bath, and sometimes she made
her teddy talk.

She also drew pictures.
She told Pam she had drawn
a picture of daddy
with a big cigar.

There was a toy library near Ann's house.
Pam sometimes met Ann and mummy there.
Ann talked to her about the toys
she would get for the next week.
Ann loved going to the clinic every week.
It was such fun.

The End